SOME

DIVINE

COMMOTION

SOME DIVINE COMMOTION

poems by

David Denny

Shanti Arts Publishing

Brunswick, Maine

Published by Shanti Arts Publishing
Interior and cover design by Shanti Arts Designs

Cover and interior image : Copyright © silm / 123rf.com

Shanti Arts LLC
193 Hillside Road,
Brunswick, Maine 04011
shantiarts.com

Printed in the United States of America

ISBN: 978-1-947067-18-9 (softcover)
ISBN: 978-1-947067-19-6 (digital)

Library of Congress Control Number: 2017961898

For Jill . . .

> *I cast my sad nets*
> *towards your ocean-blue eyes*
> *(Neruda)*

Also by David Denny —

The Gill Man in Purgatory
Man Overboard
Fool in the Attic
Plebeian on the Front Porch

Contents

ONE

The Absinthe Drinkers 14

Woman in a Purple Coat 15

The Chief Gardener in Retirement 16

Apocalyptic Charlton Heston 17

Body Double 19

Devouring Marilyn 21

Torch Song for Peter Lorre 23

Call Me Virgil 25

Headlines from a Private Tabloid 28

Suburban Scene 29

New Philosophy 31

Korah, Son of Izhar 32

Colony Collapse Disorder 33

Strong Umbrellas 35

Brouhaha 37

TWO

Zen and the Art of Loneliness 42

Sometimes Even the Angels Get It Wrong 44

The Owl Follows the River to Paradise 45

A Vast Cosmos of Shiny Things 47

Weeping a Mote Around Ben Franklin 49

Walking with Wordsworth, Punching with Papa 51

Zig-Zagging Down Lombard Street 53

Baudelaire Buzzes the Gorilla Compound 54

Our Groovy West Coast Necropolis 56

Parable of the Seed Packets 57

Aphrodite's Shower Drum Song 59

With the Devil You Never Know 60

Blue Plate Special for the Whole Wide World 62
What Lord Byron and the Diggers Do 64
Pineapple Wedges That Just Keep Coming 65
Godzilla vs. Bigfoot: A Monster Mash 67
The Ghost at the Bottom of the Well 68
Still Life with Winchester 70
Neither Notebook nor Bottle 71
Beneath the Eucalyptus Beats an Ashen Heart 72

THREE

Hikers, Three Varieties 76
Awake at 3 A.M. 78
When the Children Were Young 79
Local Habitations 80
Love Poem 81
Prayer for a Marriage 84
After a Hard Rain 85
Rats in the Attic 87
Summer School 88
Drought Orison 90
Day Hike 91
How to Paint Clouds 93
Getting the Moon Right 94
Cantankerous 95
Auto Bison 97

FOUR

To Catch a Nebbish 100
Harvest Moon 102
Clowder Cloister 103

Man Bites Dog 105

Foot Massage 107

Mating Ritual 109

No Problem 110

Household Pairs 112

Emotional Water-boarding 114

Natural Selection 116

No Diva She 117

With a Little Help from Van Gogh 119

Bitter/Sweet 121

Put Some Bleachers Out in the Sun 123

I'll See You in My Dreams 124

Acknowledgments *127*

About the Author *129*

One

The Absinthe Drinkers

On a painting by Jean-Francois Raffaelli

Later, in the asylum, as green spiders
crawl beneath your skin and the walls
ooze blood, you remember this day at
the café with Jules as "the last good day."

There you are, raising the glass
to your lips, pouring the wormwood
down your burning gullet, savoring
the fire all the way to the belly.

There is a moment just before
the Green Fairy turns Demon,
a moment between freedom and slavery,
when the air is pure and sweet,

the city is baptized in light, and your
companion the most amiable chap in town.
It is the stationmaster's final whistle.
Ahead lay the tunnel's grimy darkness;

any light therein glows only from
the pale green glass at your elbow. And
you there in the depths of your solitary
room, unable to resist its shrill summons.

Woman in a Purple Coat

On a painting by Henri Matisse

She takes her position on the divan
like all those before her. She lies back
in her garishly striped purple coat,
the clasps unfastened like the clasps
over my heart. Bold strokes of green,
red, and yellow surround her. Her eyes
shine forth like the Gorgons of old.
Warm and defiant. She is lovely;
she is dangerous. Modern and ancient.
She is the siren; she is the black widow.
Come hither and keep your distance.
A bowl of fruit, a bunch of flowers,
a reclining woman: ripe, fragrant, deadly.
Down the canvas the great swath of her
purple coat, unfastened like the clasps
over my own heart. *Pain passes*, said Renoir,
beauty remains. Green, red, yellow.
The room tilts; my head spins. She lies back
on the divan. Her eyes invite; her eyes accuse.
She signals the Emperor to have my head . . .
the purple coat unfastened like the clasps
over my battered, half-devoured heart.

The Chief Gardener in Retirement

My granddaughter leads me by the hand through
the big oval rooms at Musée de l'Orangerie.
Once again I stand among the lilies I planted
so long ago. I do indeed feel as though
I were back in Giverny, as they all said I would.
The pictures recall for me the dank, ripe odors:

the algae and the mud and the floral bouquet.
I miss the song birds and the smell of bread
baking in the humid kitchen next to my shed.
I even miss the insects with their steady hum.
I close my eyes and see the old man perched
with his easel on our famous bridge, squinting

at the water. Behind his back we mocked his
royal arrogance. We hated him. We admired him.
It was I who called forth the color and the light —
I who lay the blues and the greens, the pinks
and the reds at his feet. But it was he, only he,
who captured them in shimmering strokes of oil.

I open my eyes, slowly turn, and turn again.
Even from the grave his mastery chastens me.
And even now I am lifted by his vision.
Other painters have come and gone. None
to make us feel that we breathe the sacred air
of that first bright morning in paradise.

Apocalyptic Charlton Heston

More cynical and clammy than Western Heston or
Moses Heston or even Judah Ben-Hur Heston,
Apocalyptic Heston is anti-epic, much less likely
to strike the Northwestern University-trained
acting school pose — that smug you'll-soon-find-out-
I'm-the-hero-of-this-picture pose — remnant
from the age of Barrymore and Fairbanks.
Apocalyptic Heston is a scavenger, a roamer,
a Duke gone rogue, cut loose from the hero's
code by rampant, empirical, planet-devouring
capitalism and spun into his own oxygen-depleted
hyper-Darwinian filmic orbit. Apocalyptic Heston has
little of the sonorous America-first Bible-recitation
Heston of his later years. Even the rifle-raising
pry-it-I-dare-you-from-my-cold-dead-fingers
NRA Heston, for all its Republican posturing,
wouldn't survive in a room with Apocalyptic Heston,
whose Dudley Do-Right chin is bruised,
stubble-covered, and weary of humanity's
death-loving hubris. He may be lugging a weapon,
but it's clear from the haphazard way it's slung
over his shoulder that it doesn't have a name.
He only cleans it because there's nothing else
to do and no one to talk to — they've all been
swallowed up by the great earthquake, crushed
into protein-rich crackers, or ravaged by mutant
cells no immune system but his could battle.
It's not that he's lost his humanity, but he has
dropped the now burdensome and obsolete load
of decorum required by the late great western civilization.

He can still fall to his knees in the sand,
shedding tears of rage and sadness for what's
been lost, but the camera is very far away
and the sobs are drowned out by the elegiac strains
of Montovani's violin-heavy score. Indeed,
absent Cecil B. DeMille production values,
Apocalyptic Heston has his own brand of sweaty
1970s cinemascope appeal. But no Orange County
nomination committee would ask him to run
for office. No AFI tributes for him. No tuxedos
or red carpet strolls. No late-night TV guest
appearances with amusing behind-the-scenes
anecdotes. Not even Michael Moore would dare
satirize him for fear of Apocalyptic Heston's
nothing-left-to-lose reprisal. Alzheimer's
wouldn't dare stalk him. Apocalyptic Heston's
long goodbye is a medium shot at dusk;
he's standing alone on the rubble heap of
a Malibu mansion, turning over chunks of chimney
debris with his steel-toed boot. Don't expect him
to wave as the camera cranes back and
the credits roll. His eyes are fixed on some
far-away vanishing point on the horizon,
lit by the lavender atmospheric pollution
that gives this finale its tragic luster as the painted
cyclorama sun sinks slowly into the Pacific.

Body Double

Marli Renfro stood in for Janet Leigh in the
infamous shower scene of Hitchcock's Psycho

I was the girl who didn't mind taking off her clothes.
It's easy to be a nudist before gravity begins its cruel tricks.
So when that pale, loose-jowled British sow bug
offered me $500 to strip and stand in a fake shower
while he photographed me up and down and every
which way, I told my boss I'd be back in a week and
hopped aboard the chartered Hollywood-bound studio jet.

Frankly, I expected the usual pinch and tickle.
He never touched me. Just sat there in his director's chair,
leering, whispering directions to the cameraman.
Even the hot studio lights didn't bother me. I'm a desert girl,
after all; it takes a lot to make me sweat. Like Hef,
Hitch was just another dirty old Puritan with money
enough to make his tootsies twist and pout.

When I finally saw the movie, I couldn't believe how
fast the whole scene flew, what with his fancy cuts
from frame to frantic frame, and the violin's hawk
scream as the knife came down and down. Somewhere
in Hollywood there is a vault with cans and cans
of footage of me standing, squatting, squirming,
and turning in that damned fiberglass tank of his.

In Vegas the following Tuesday, it was back to the old
bump and grind. At least the club was air-conditioned
and my dressing room private. And when I posed for
the nudie mags the photographers bought me lunch.
There's no lonelier place on earth than Soundstage Six
at Universal Studios when the crew breaks for lunch
without so much as a thank you ma'am and here's your robe.

I never met Janet. I hear she's nice. She certainly has
a great figure. I suppose it was something of a compliment
to be her tits and ass for a week. I did meet Tony Perkins
one night. He came backstage after our show.
"You dance beautifully," he said. Such a tender, delicate boy,
with a wide grin and narrow shoulders. Those lovely
dark eyes that Hitch turned into the devil's own.

In the desert we get these flash electrical storms, where
the heat and humidity build and build. The clouds darken;
a heavy silence hovers, and then the sky breaks open,
and water — you can't believe how much water — pours down
from God's own spigot, soaking everything until
the broad sidewalks of the strip run like a river,
ruining convertibles, washing clean all our residual sin.

Maybe *Psycho* was like that: enough pressure built up
behind it that when it burst forth in a sudden rush
of sex and death, it felt like something of a miracle,
like water flowing through parched land, filling reservoirs
that had long stood empty. Well, what do I know?
All that's left me is saggy tortoise skin, two dead husbands,
an Airstream that keeps me cool and dry, and this story.

Devouring Marilyn

In the summer of 1947, Norma Jeane Mortenson was crowned Artichoke Queen of Castroville, California

Beware the sharp barbs at the tip of each leaf.
It is wise to clip them before steaming.
Marilyn's nipples are talons. With them,
by the light of a honey moon, she shreds
poor Joseph Cotten's heart. Yours too, friend.
Mariners, beware this Muse of the lower world.
Her enchantments entice and enslave.

The outer leaves are tough and fibrous.
Only the small pith where the leaf attaches
is edible. Dipped in butter and scraped across
the lower teeth, Marilyn tastes better than
Jane Russell. Go tell Howard Hawks that when
Marilyn swings her hips, she reveals the secret
place where her soul attaches to her body.

The inner leaves are tender and entirely edible.
Strumming Bob Mitchum's guitar, Marilyn lulls
toads and whippoorwills down the valley. You hear
the wild river roar beneath her fragile melody.
Try to hum along. Butter or no, it is this tenderness
under the toughness that draws you into peril,
carries you dangerously close to the rocky shoal.

The choke is fine, fuzzy, with hair-like filaments.
Go ahead and store your underwear in the freezer.
Tom Ewell stands-in for all those tied to the mast.
As the subway breeze lifts Marilyn's skirt,
the train rumbles beneath your dreams, and
Billy Wilder's demonic laughter is heard on the wind.
How many yet cry out for the remedy?

The meaty, succulent center is called the heart.
Divide it as you will, into bite-sized pieces.
Wilder uses a hot saxophone and Tony Curtis
in glasses to bring Marilyn to her peak.
Draw that pink boa across your lonely shoulders.
Only the deaf, dumb, and blind could resist her plea
to be loved by you and nobody else but you.

The stem is a stringy outer layer with a meaty center.
Neither Clark Gable nor Monty Clift could free
Marilyn from the moon-drawn tides of Nembutal.
Like Arthur Miller, you think you might save her.
Not many know this: the artichoke thistle
is a blood relative of the sunflower, whose lovely
face follows the sun across the summer sky.

Torch Song for Peter Lorre

Come to me, my melancholy baby.
Cuddle up and don't be blue.
All your fears are foolish fancy, maybe.
You know dear that I'm in love with you.
    — George Norton

She discovered him lurking backstage
in Berlin. She named him, nudged him
towards the footlights, warmed him,

slapped his sallow cheeks, whispered
secrets that moistened his soft brown
cow eyes. She sent him to Brecht. She

sent him to Fritz Lang. She sent him
to Hitchcock and to America. She
allowed him sips from her goblet

of pale nectar: Love and Success
followed. She endowed him with enough
wit to sit among literati and politicos.

She told him no one would ever
love him like her, like her. Dark
nectar, too, she gave him to drink —

Ambition and Lust followed. She
crooned him a ghoulish pick-up line
to use on starlets around the studio:

"Do you think you could get used
to my body?" She placed a pistol
in his sweaty palm to point at Bogie.

She raised him (the Obsequious Scoundrel
par excellence) before she lowered him
into the warm pool of mediocrity,

where the single requirement is
steady refinement of that gentle art,
self-parody. She bloated him.

She boogey-manned him. She guided
him towards bankruptcy. She enticed him
with a return trip to Europe. Last,

she rode him through the sunbaked
streets of Roger Corman's Hollywood,
drove a banderilla into his fat neck.

Spreading lotus blossoms over his pale
corpse, she thrummed a familiar tune
(while I kiss away each tear, my dear):

Told him no one had ever loved him
like her, like her. Told him no one
had ever, ever loved him like her.

Call Me Virgil

Hop in the backseat of my beat up Prius. Agent for
Shadow-world Real Estate, I'll show you the house
you never want to buy. The diamond-shaped yellow sign
out front of 22272 Cupertino Road says "Dead End."
In fact, when Ray Carver lived here in 1972, he was poised
at the top of his slippery alcoholic slope. The steady rain
of whiskey and cheap vodka turned the soil beneath him
to mud. It would not be long before he could gain
no foothold at all. The remainder of the decade
would be one long, slow, bleary-eyed spiral descent.

It was here, in this house, that his marriage
to Maryanne dissolved, here that their two teenage
children were left to raise themselves, and here
that drinking emerged as his main occupation.
Still, he managed a few hours a week to work
on the stories and poems that had begun to bring him
notoriety. It was under such circumstances that he
adopted the motto of Isak Dinesen, who spoke
from a 3 x 5 card tacked to the wall above his typewriter:
"Write a little each day, without hope and without despair."

Someone else lives here now. Their old heap
sits at the end of the driveway, tires low, roof rusted.
Ray, too, had trouble with cars. He was forever trying to
lose one that had broken down and find one that wouldn't.
When he won the first of his big literary awards,
he went right out and bought a new one. It was a sign
of something, that first new car. His luck had turned.

Life would indeed be different now that he could
just slide onto the leather upholstery, turn the key,
and go wherever he damn well wanted to go.

The house is no longer blue, but the dilapidated
wagon wheel still leans against the front of the car port —
somebody's idea of a decorative touch. Late on certain
summer nights, when it was too hot to sleep and Ray
was too drunk to write, he would step out onto the lawn,
lean against this wagon wheel, listen to the crickets
in the olive tree, and gaze up at the foothills.
Clouds obscured the moon, then they separated, filling
the patchy lawn with a soft circle of light. If I could
step back onto that lawn with him, what would I say?

I'd have to admit that things would grow even worse
for a time. He was about to slide uncontrollably
down that muddy slope, after all. But I might
let him know that the present misery would not last.
I would not tell him how hard and how quickly
his life would swerve. Then swerve again.
I would not say outright that love would save him,
that the thing he would be most proud of, in the end,
would be that he quit drinking. On such a summer's
night, who could stomach such a fairytale?

Gazing at the foothills, I might think out loud
about how much this place would change.

Ray could not afford to buy his old house now that
this valley is named for silicon rather than an Italian saint.
Hang on, I might say. And despite Isak Dinesen,
I might encourage him to accept the moment when
the midsummer moon sidesteps the clouds as a sign that
mercy arrives at the most unexpected moments, that
it's possible to trade one life for another, to slide into it,
turn the key, and drive where it is you really want to go.

Headlines from a Private Tabloid

Man Seeks Ultimate Meaning of Universe,
      Settles for Sitcoms and Chocolates

Father's Teeth Crumble in Mouth,
      Spits Enamel Shards at Disobedient Children

Woman Loves Same Man for Sixteen Lifetimes,
      Guru Cites Cosmological Malfunction

Soccer Mom Drinks Starbucks Dry,
      Coffee Mogul Demands Death Penalty

Woman Chews Left Ear Off George Clooney,
      Claims It Smelled of Cinnamon

Northwest Bigfoot Cave Discovered,
      Walls Covered with Stolen Picassos

Two-Headed Nun Chants in Latin and Martian,
      Pope Declares Interplanetary Miracle

Housecat awakens after eight-year coma:
      "I could hear rats in the floor boards at night"

Celebrity Psychic Channels Richard Burton:
      "I still love Liz, that six-timing Jezebel!"

Novelist Admits Plagiarism: "I Sampled Chandler
      and Tolstoy and No One Even Noticed!"

Suburban Scene

The mountain lion sleeps in the sycamore.
He is first spotted by the jogger, who calls
the sheriff, who calls the game warden.
They stand now at a safe distance while
the animal twitches and the great black-tipped
tail sweeps. He is stretched out across
a heavy horizontal branch where trail turns
sidewalk. Nearby a plaque lists the names
of the city council who sanctioned this paving.

Cars slow. Neighbors gather and whisper.
No one asks what has brought the creature
down into the land of poodles and dachshunds,
to the level ground of trash trucks and school
buses, backpacks and briefcases. Like the
skinny deer who come to sip at the creek,
the drought has drawn him down from the hills.

The warden considers his options. 180 pounds,
he guesses, of tawny muscle and claws and jaws.
When he awakens it will be to prowl and stalk
and devour. The cop thinks of his two-year-old
standing naked in the kiddie pool. The neighbors
notice the strong musky tang, how it lingers
in the absence of breeze. How long has this
beast been snoozing among us? What havoc
will awaken when he springs to the ground?

The warden slides a tranquilizer dart into
his rifle. The cop cracks open his shotgun
and loads both barrels. The neighbors take
another step back from the caution tape,
point their camera phones as the lion stirs,
yawns, stretches. Dusk soon. The cool
darkness calls. His yellow eyes blink open,
survey the hunting ground, rich with prey.

New Philosophy

The best way to learn Paris, she said, is to get lost.
Hop on the Metro and observe commuters,
tourists, schoolchildren, immigrants. Emerge
from the tunnels expecting nothing. Stroll through
an unfamiliar district. Browse its shops. Buy
some small item you don't need. Eat something.
If it rains, duck beneath an awning and drink
whatever they set before you. If someone asks you
a question, strike up a conversation. Forget
whatever you've learned. You're truly lost now,
and no amount of pre-acquired knowledge can help.
Repeat this routine, day by day, until you have a map
in your head. About the time you begin to feel
the city is yours, leave it. Lose it. Find a new city,
a city no one has ever visited. Get lost. Live this way
until you find yourself no longer alive. Let them
look for you, if they like, in the corners of doorways,
in alleys, beneath every bridge ever erected over
every river that ever flowed through your aching heart.

Korah, Son of Izhar

He was dreaming of a dog romping in a field.
It did not resemble a dog he had ever owned,
yet in the dream the dog was definitely his.
He had thrown a ball into the field and the dog
was searching among the weeds. He whistled
and the dog's ears perked. He heard a low rumble
coming from beyond the dark barrier of the treeline.
He awoke of a sudden as his bed lurched and leapt.
The roar was not an approaching train,
though it may as well have been. The earth
beneath his bedroom gave way, revealing
a cavernous hole into which his bed dropped.
He thought he should scream. Perhaps he did
scream. If so, it would not have been heard
above the growl of the earth as she opened her throat.
Was she howling? Far away, someone whistled
and called his name. There was a ball hidden
somewhere. His task was to fetch it and return
before the darkness swallowed him whole.

Colony Collapse Disorder

Everywhere this scene repeats itself: The keeper
turns his pick up into the clearing, stands over
the empty boxes, raises the bill of his cap and
looks into the sky above the tree line. He yanks
open the boxes and one-by-one pulls the cedar
frames from the hives. A few stragglers buzz
aimlessly around him. He examines the wax.
He searches the immediate area for dead bees.
He tosses the empties into the bed of his truck
and hauls them to an open field where the discards
pile up. He will have to burn them, bonfire-style.

All over, bees are leaving and they aren't coming
back. No one knows why. Some think it may be
pesticides — like sin, poisoning unto the fourth
generation. But no one really knows why the bees
are leaving the hives — those famously sophisticated
monarchies, a social order so beautiful in their
symmetrical structure they were once used
to illustrate the Great Chain of Being: every
creature a secure place, a particular task, a purpose

to fulfill under the matriarch's beneficent gaze.
Everywhere the mystery replicates: parents and
children, husbands and wives simply walk away
from the intricate scaffolding of their lives:
a single mind comes undone, a family dissolves,
a society shivers in the dark, and the shadows
of ash and maple sway in the slight breeze made
by the bonfire's flames. Homes and businesses,

churches and hospitals, pubs and shops stand empty
while keepers search for corpses. No one has
a convincing explanation. Something strange
in the water? Has the air itself been altered?
Some sub-lethal pathogen lurking in our cells?

All over, this leaving without returning. If this be
liberation, where are the manifestos? Where
the sign-carrying hoards marching on important
public buildings? Where the revolutionary poems
of discontent? The utopian visionaries and their
passionate visions? Only this leaving without
returning. The mystery of it. The strange new reality
of empty hives, bulging only with waxy remnants,
the piles of empty boxes awaiting the splash
of kerosene, the spark of the keeper's match.

Strong Umbrellas

Drum fish wash ashore on the banks
of the Arkansas River.
Thousands of rotting fish corpses
bump against each other
along its crusty banks. Blackbirds fall
from the sky in Little Rock.
Thousands of blackbirds hit
the asphalt, like those people
in the Twin Towers after
the planes hit — people who,
in their frantic final moments,
decided they would rather fly
than burn. A blackbird smashes
the windshield of a state cruiser.
The Little Rock police chief jokes
that we need strong umbrellas
to defend against the onslaught.
It took the firemen in the lobby
of the South Tower a moment
to interpret the strange sound
of bodies hitting the pavement outside.
It gave them pause
before they adjusted their gear
and charged up the emergency
staircases. That day, planes fell
from the sky; people tried
like hell to outrun debris clouds.
The sanctuaries where stories
of God's compassion are passed

still stand tall. His grand silence
echoes, sends us to our knees.
Drum fish bump against the blank
river's shore. Blackbirds fall
from the sky in central Arkansas.
Did you hear of the unexplained
shower of apples that rained
upon a small town near London?
Or the large metallic ball that
dropped on a remote grassland
in Namibia? They say it was
two symmetrical halves welded
perfectly together, that it was hollow
and did not explode. How about
the eerie frog falls and
the maggot downpour in Acapulco?
I'm trying not to fall
for the conspiracy theories,
trying not to see these things
as apocalyptic menu items.
Grab that large black umbrella,
friend, the one with the ivory handle,
the one with the iron ribs.
Yes, spring it open, please.
Walk by my side and cover us both.

Brouhaha

Scorching July afternoon. Chavez Ravine.
Middle of game two, double-header.
Players drowsy. Spotty crowd slunk beneath
caps and sunglasses. Organ music paces.
Big steroidal slugger hugs plate. Waits
for high and outside. Pitcher crouches
like a cat. Stretches. Spits. Momentarily tall
on the rubber. Lets loose. Fastball clips
steroidal slugger on left kneecap. Mass
inhalation. Silence. Slugger turns back
momentarily. Looking for someone in stands?
Jaw twitches. Pitcher freezes. Terror strikes.
Slugger turns and charges. Mad elephant.
Sudden glee on pitcher's face. Drops mitt.
Lifts fists. Body tightens. Like magnets,
slugger and pitcher clash, clash again.

Stadium seats squeak in unison. Uproar.
Both dugouts empty. Tangle of fists and
elbows, spittle and curses. A fierce tide
sweeps in: from home bench, blue and white;
from visitor's bench, red and gray.
Sultry afternoon explodes into joyous battle.
Crowd awakens, rises, shouts. Dregs of beer
and peanuts fly. Stands come alive
with rhythm. Pounding feet echo. Fight!
Great hormonal surge sweeps stadium.
Red and blue, white and gray mingle, tangle,
crash. Flurry of punches. Melee. Into the throng

black uniforms. Dodging the worst. Disentangling
the fracas. Wild and indiscriminate rage.
Madness. Hard rock through PA system.
Black uniforms prevail, prevail again.

Players tire, allow themselves to be separated.
Hullabaloo subsides. Too hot for this shit.
Fans reseat. Everybody wide awake now.
Dugouts repopulate. Gatorade flows.
Infield grass again visible. Tide wanes.
Anger becomes mere irritation. Threats
become mere insults. Caps recovered.
Brick dust slapped from thighs. Bloody noses
pinched. Shoulders shrugged. Uniforms adjusted.
Cheeks refilled with chew. Beer and peanut
vendors stream into aisles. Cold beer here.
Get your ice cold beer here! Ice cream
sandwiches. Hot dogs. Stadium settles.
Truce takes hold. Pitcher mounts rubber.
New batter in box. Middle of game two.
Chavez Ravine. Scorching July afternoon.

Two

Zen and the Art of Loneliness

Richard Brautigan feels the screen door smack him
on the butt as it bangs shut. Or is that his mother's
hand? Since his father left it has been like this.

Whenever a man comes through the front door,
Brautigan gets shooed out the back. He may
return when the man's car is gone. He grabs

his father's old rod, reel, and tackle. He sneaks
a slice of bread from the deaf woman's kitchen
next door. He follows the deer trail through

the woods, across the highway, and down
to the banks of the McKenzie. He finds
a mother lode of red worms in the moist soil

beneath the firs. He walks into the cold water
up to his knees at a place where the river runs
narrow and deep. He casts his line into the swift

current along the opposite shore. The mosquitoes
buzzing in his ears are only buzzing. Neither
the birds nor the squirrels nor the fish themselves

speak of his mother or her parade of men or
the bully who trips and taunts him on the playground.
After a while Brautigan loses track of time.

He vaguely hears the crank and grind of truck gears
back on the highway. But that is the only reminder
of that other world. His legs are numb. He casts

and casts the impaled worms into the swift current
beneath the blackberries. Just this and nothing more.
Soon he acquires a pile of glistening rainbow trout

on the shoreline. Fish enough to feed a multitude.
But there is only him, just him, a white-blond
skinny boy with a growling stomach, on the cusp

of a growth spurt, out here on the dreamy rim
of nowhere, hauling in this miraculous catch, under
the summer sun, on the west coast of America, 1947.

Sometimes Even the Angels Get It Wrong

Richard Brautigan says "once upon a time a boy
loved a girl but the girl loved somebody else"
is the story of every artist who ever wrote,

painted, sang, or whatever. We do what we do
to get that girl's attention and keep her head
from turning away. Love is the soul's caffeine.

Without it we feel listless and bored. Without love
life becomes a series of political ads for the least
charming candidate. On the Goodpasture

Covered Bridge, Dick Brautigan tries to kiss
Linda Webster. Beneath them the McKenzie River roars.
The angels in the rafters cheer. The 10 slatted

Gothic-arched windows gently guide the summer's
morning light into the sacred space. And lovely
14-year-old Linda Webster steps away from

lanky Brautigan, steps away, uninterested, perhaps
even mildly disgusted by his advance, steps away
and crosses the remainder of the bridge by herself,

leaving Richard Brautigan alone in the holy temple
of his imagination. Once upon a time a boy loved
a girl but the girl loved somebody, anybody, else.

The Owl Follows the River to Paradise

Richard Brautigan throws a rock through
the front window of the police station
in Eugene, Oregon. It is 1955. He is not

making a political statement; he is hungry.
His 19-year-old brain tells him he will be fed
in jail. The cops walk outside, scratching

their heads. *I guess we'll have to arrest you now*,
the chief says. The court orders him to 60 days
in the Oregon State Insane Asylum in Salem.

Richard Brautigan is strapped to the treatment
table and a rubber bit shoved between his teeth.
When they apply the electrodes to his temples,

the doctors and the nurses stand clear.
His 19-year-old body convulses and seizes.
Later he compares it to the famous scene

in *Frankenstein* when the monster is animated
during an electrical storm. A nurse dabs the drool
from the corners of his mouth as she removes

the bit. The psychiatrist pats his thigh.
Richard, he says, *you're going to be just fine*.
His 19-year-old brain repeats: *I'm going to be*

just fine. He sleeps and sleeps. When he wakes
they bring him a tray of food. By God he eats it, too,
sensing the lean years ahead. It is at this point

that he begins to fly. He is skinny enough to
squeeze through the window bars. He soars
over the rolling green hills around the hospital

like a spotted owl, skimming the tops of fir trees
until he finds the river. He follows the river
south, towards California, towards the source

of the books he has carried in his back pocket
all through his youth. He is going to be just fine.
He was hungry and imprisoned, and now he is free.

A Vast Cosmos of Shiny Things

Richard Brautigan sits at a corner table
in Café Trieste, sipping a cappuccino and
watching the North Beach parade pass

on the sidewalk, a tall stack of new books
at his elbow. He has spent the morning
in City Lights, combing the shelves, listening

for the voices of old and new friends.
The milk foam clings to his moustache.
He opens a shiny new paperback and

begins to read. His moustache starts to
harden and crust. It turns into a clump
of cauliflower right there on his lip. Soon

mushrooms sprout from his ears,
and the hair on his head becomes broccoli.
From each shoulder springs a daisy.

Lawrence Ferlinghetti, Allen Ginsberg, and
Jack Kerouac walk in. They take a table
in the shade of Brautigan's garden.

Kerouac picks a daisy and places it
into Ginsberg's beard. Ferlinghetti breaks off
a piece of Brautigan's moustache

and pops it into his mouth.
It is just another day in San Francisco,
a mostly human habitation on the eastern

rim of the Pacific Ocean, in the northern
hemisphere of Earth, a blue planet in
the Milky Way, a singular galaxy among

many in a universe among many
in the vast cosmos of shiny things
and dark, seemingly empty spaces.

Weeping a Mote Around Ben Franklin

Richard Brautigan circles Washington Square Park
on his hickory broomstick. It is 1961 and
the sun is shining all over America.

He does not cackle, no. He flies in silence,
watching the children play in the sandbox,
watching the nuns across the street at

the Church of Saints Peter and Paul, watching
the old Italians chew cigars and play poker.
He comes in for a landing and fills his belly

at the public drinking fountain. But now
he is too water-logged to fly. He kneels
at the base of the statue of Benjamin Franklin,

who looks down upon him with a grim smile,
his three-cornered hat tucked under
his left arm, a book in his right hand.

Richard Brautigan weeps when the conductor
of the Mason Street cable car clangs his bell
and everyone reaches for a strap as the car

lurches up the hill. He weeps as Ben Franklin
recalls for him the April day in 1956 when
Joe DiMaggio and Marilyn Monroe posed for

pictures on the steps of the church following
their wedding. He weeps at the memory of the poem
that got away that morning, the one he thought

sure he'd set his hook into, the poem that swam
to freedom up Geary Street and out of sight.
He weeps a mote around Ben Franklin.

Finally, he mounts his hickory broomstick
and speaks the magic words. He pushes off
from the sidewalk and glides over the poplars,

circling back over Franklin, who winks
at him, places his three-cornered hat
atop his bald head, and hops down from

his cement perch, joining the old Italians
in a game of poker, jokers and deuces wild,
play at your own risk, winner take nothing.

Walking with Wordsworth, Punching with Papa

Richard Brautigan stands in the cold rush
of Big Smoky Creek. The biggest fish
are holding in a deep pool next to the boulders,

just beyond his reach. He aims his rod
in their direction, flicking his wrist in one
fluid motion as lure and line whip and whip

through the crisp morning air of July 2, 1961.
Straddling a log on the shore, his wife and baby
daughter follow the jaunty rhythm of Brautigan's

fiberglass RA Special. On the floor of the Plymouth
station wagon, beneath the borrowed Royal typer,
lies the manuscript that will change everything

and nothing. 40 miles away, in Ketchum,
Ernest Hemingway places the blue double barrel
of his W & C Scott shotgun to his forehead and

trips the trigger. Brautigan catches his limit,
and he catches a cold. Summer is all but over.
Any day now they will break camp and drive

back to San Francisco. It's been said that
Wordsworth's verse comes at a walker's pace.
Hemingway's best prose bobs and punches

like a cornered prize fighter. Richard Brautigan's
style captures the pulse of a man knee-deep
in an icy river, his arm flexing out and back

as he reaches and reaches for the biggest trout,
the ones holding in the swiftest current,
in the deepest pool, just beyond reach.

Zig-Zagging Down Lombard Street

Richard Brautigan's sadness goes down smooth
as hot buttered rum. It flushes his veins with
quicksilver and blossoms into multi-colored

tattoos of flowers and butterflies and peace symbols.
Under a black light his skin glows like a
phosphorescent algae bloom on the Sea of Japan.

Once upon a moonless night he swims
to Alcatraz accompanied by fog horns and
drunken sailor shanties. The ghosts of death row

prisoners blaze in memory of their executions.
The ghost of Governor Pat Brown offers no
clemency. Nevertheless, 13 sea lions hail taxis

and ride them to the top of Russian Hill,
where they bark love poems to unrequited
tourists zig-zagging down Lombard Street.

Baudelaire Buzzes the Gorilla Compound

Richard Brautigan is seated at the IBM Selectric
in his small apartment on Geary Street.
It is one hour before dusk in the year 1963.

He is *tick-tack-ticking* the keys in the same
soulful manner that Thelonious Monk plays
the piano ... *tick-tack-tickety-tack*. He lifts

his hands. He goes to the window and lights
a cigarette. He tells Robert Creeley to play
the Selectric for awhile. He opens the window

and leaps. Robert Creeley plays Richard
Brautigan's Selectric while he flies around
the neighborhood ... *tickety-tack-tick-tick-tack*.

As long as Creeley keeps playing, Brautigan remains
airborne. If Creeley stops, Brautigan will fall ...
tick-tack-tickety-tack-tack-ding!-tack-tack-tack.

Eventually Richard Brautigan flies back
in the open window. He lands on his feet and
straightens his windblown hair. He adjusts

his glasses and closes the window. He pulls on
his old gray sweater with the patches on the elbows.
He walks over to the Selectric, releases

the carriage lock, and pulls out the sheet.
Creeley has typed a poem entitled "Flight,"
in which Brautigan, disguised as Baudelaire,

loops the towers of the Golden Gate Bridge,
buzzes the gorilla compound at the zoo,
swoops down to the take-out window of

the Dairy Queen and grabs a soft serve
vanilla cone dipped in chocolate and peanuts.
Richard Brautigan grabs a pencil. *We need*

a comma here, he says. He straightens, then
bends again to the paper. *No, nevermind*.
He rubs the eraser and blows free its

tiny debris. He tucks the pencil behind an ear.
Robert Creeley carries two ice-filled glasses
from the kitchen. Richard Brautigan fills them

with bourbon. They raise their glasses and silently
toast the fog as it circles the building twice, and
rubs its purple whiskers against the window pane.

Our Groovy West Coast Necropolis

Richard Brautigan stands among tombstones
in the Presidio Pet Cemetery. The gravemarkers
say Fifi, Congo, Rex. The graveyard is ringed

by a whitewashed picket fence. Brautigan's
white-blond hair shines in the summer sunlight.
Beneath his feet lay the bones of Reno, Quincy,

Skippy. Beyond the fence — mature pine,
cypress, eucalyptus. He is scribbling into
a small notebook. Patsy, Linus, Pug.

Wildflowers bloom among the headstones:
red, yellow, blue. Brautigan's hair the eternal
flame in this animal Arlington of the west.

Tippy, Cleo, Lucky. He wriggles his bare toes
in the dirt. A chorus of barks and mews
seeps through the soft soil. Laddie, Sassy, Mixup.

Parable of the Seed Packets

Richard Brautigan gives away seed packets
on the street corners of San Francisco,
seed packets with his poems printed on the

envelope under the title *Please Plant These Poems:*
carrots, Shasta daisy, squash, lettuce, parsley,
sweet alyssum, and a mixture of California

wild flowers. So you see, you can eat Richard
Brautigan or you can just admire his colorful
and fragrant beauty. Some of the seeds fall

upon concrete, where they roll down the steep
hillsides and into the bay and out under the bridge
and into the swift currents of the great Pacific,

where they are lost to us forever but food
for some sad creature of the deep. And
some of the seeds are planted in hip pockets

or macramé purses or knapsacks and sprout
only much later as sweet welcome home kisses
or hot soup and sourdough lunches or guitar

picking verses. And some of the seeds are
taken up by whiffs of thick fog blowing in
off the bay and are carried over land far and

wide, taking root in soil containing the rich
bonemeal of Mastadons and ancient sharks
and your sweet aunt Betsy from Pike.

They grow willy-nilly and provide shade
from the heat of the day and comfort
in the loneliest part of the night. Seeds.

Packets of seeds. Richard Brautigan gives
away packets of seeds and poems on
the street corners of San Francisco, 1967.

Aphrodite's Shower Drum Song

Richard Brautigan says the price of free love
is too high in this inflation economy. Once
he received a great blow job from a woman

who spat his gism into her hand and proclaimed
in wonder, "Richard Brautigan's sperm!"
He was farther out than anyone thought,

and not singing but sighing. They say Eros
wounded himself with his own weapon
while wooing Psyche. Turned down

one night on Haight Street, Brautigan
kicked in the car door of the woman
who rejected him. "Maniac!" she screamed,

as she tore away from the curb. Hey, Nonny,
Nonny, Dick Brautigan was much too far out
all his life, and not singing but sighing.

With the Devil You Never Know

Richard Brautigan walks backwards down
Pacific Coast Highway, a knapsack slung over
his shoulder, his thumb pointed at the sky.

10,000 cars pass him by before a brand new
Mercedes Benz pulls over. Brautigan slides
into the passenger seat. You're late, he says.

The driver answers, I'm always late, but
I always show. What have you got for me?
Brautigan opens his knapsack and rummages.

I have the Devil's own back-up singers.
These 3 girls can curl your toes with their
harmonies. I have a grand suspension bridge

built of fog and rainbow droppings. It'll get you
safely across any relatively stagnant body of water.
And I have 30 over-inflated weather balloons

filled with helium and joy. They'll lift you
out of any dilemma and set you down in a field
of poppies in the county of your own choosing.

The Mercedes speeds on down the highway.
The sky is cerulean, the curling waves are teal
and Payne's gray, the sunset clouds are a pale

magenta tinged with lemon yellow. I have
my share of troubles, the driver says,
but I'm afraid of heights. I'd love to sink

my toes into those rainbow droppings, but
I've already got a suspension bridge in the back
of the tour bus. I'll be traveling with Big Brother

and the Holding Company this summer, and
I could sure use some kick-ass back-up singers.
I imagine there's a contract for me to sign?

Always, Richard Brautigan replies. I warn you,
you never know how long you'll get.
Some get a decade, some only a single year

before the Devil comes to collect. Give me
the pen, she says, pulling over into the sand,
I'll sign. Just give me the god-damned pen.

Blue Plate Special for the Whole Wide World

Richard Brautigan fishes in the icy stream
that runs past his Montana ranch, taking four
big rainbow trout for a bounty. He splits

the fish with his knife and cleans them,
scraping the scales and leaving the heads
and fins for the scavengers. Back at the ranch,

he fries them in butter and lemon and a shot
of whiskey. He salts and peppers the fish.
He lays them on a big blue plate on the kitchen

table. He opens wide the front door and
invites the whole world in for lunch.
We file in and each take a bite of that fine,

juicy, nourishing trout. So sweet and so delicious.
As we chew and swallow, we think,
Well, this life is good. We are meant to be here.

This is our world, after all. We are not
strangers. This is our fish, our ranch,
our Montana, our America, our Earth.

We file outside with satisfied bellies.
And some of us take flight, and some of us swim
downstream, towards the river, towards the sea,

and some of us mount horses, riding
in all directions, and some light out on foot,
with only our good sense and a sturdy pair

of boots to carry us — that and the stories twirling
in our noggins like small ballerinas
dancing on the stage of our minds.

What Lord Byron and the Diggers Do

Richard Brautigan says fame sparkles and flits
like an elegant fly, luring its victim into
the shallows. It appears a delicious morsel,

a feathery jewel, a piece of the sun. Few can
refuse it. Once swallowed, its hidden barbs
tear and twist the ego into a bloody mass,

shredding its host from the inside out.
Brautigan says let your curly locks grow.
Let your love beads hang just so. Go on

and snap your fingers to the beat. May as well
carpe that diem. Make drink not merry.
Eat, love, be war. Drizzle pop, drizzle pop.

On the shore his tail flops, his gills breathe
in the terrible oxygen of success. Go on and
drizzle, drizzle pop, yes, drizzle pop, pop.

Pineapple Wedges That Just Keep Coming

Richard Brautigan says happiness is possible
in this life, yet it is elusive, and it may not be
approached directly, but perhaps it may be

wooed with a certain kind of chocolates and
flowers and, of course, wine of a favorable vintage.
It is unwise to sneak up on happiness in hopes

of scaring it into our arms; it is by nature
skittish and suspicious and a terribly fast sprinter.
Richard Brautigan says don't even bother

with happiness; best not to even acknowledge it.
If we're lucky it may follow us home, like a tramp
dog that smells something tasty on our shoe.

It is a waste of mental energy to consider happiness;
all your best theorizing leads only down a drab
cul de sac of material comfort and spiritual yearning.

Richard Brautigan says throw an existence party
and don't even invite happiness. Be resolute
about this, even if it shows up in a tux asking

to use the bathroom. Many have brought it
inside under such a pretense. It makes noise
in there, whistling and running water

in the sink, as if it were a satisfied guest.
Do not be fooled by such chicanery.
Richard Brautigan says only later, after

hours of polite knocking and eventually
picking the lock with a hairpin, would we
discover the little window above the bathtub

jimmied wide open and happiness out walking
the lonely streets again with head down, hands
shoved deeply in pockets, daydreaming of

a tropical paradise — chaise lounge propped
in the sand and neon blue drinks festooned
with pineapple wedges that just keep coming.

Godzilla vs. Bigfoot: A Monster Mash

Richard Brautigan wanders the streets of Tokyo,
ducks into porn theaters, scribbles a thousand
stories into his small notebook. When he insults

another drunken writer at The Cradle one night,
the man breaks his nose. Bloody, stewed, confused,
Brautigan stumbles out towards Tokyo Bay.

Godzilla rises from the roiling water
while ten thousand Japanese run screaming
through the streets. The monster roars

its atomic breath, transforming Brautigan
into a Shinto god of destruction. Later, Brautigan
invites a crowd to his Montana ranch

for a spaghetti feed and ping-pong tournament.
Bigfoot watches from the woods behind
the big redwood barn. After his wife Akiko

beats him in the final round, Brautigan takes
an ax to the table, reducing it to splinters.
Slurping leftover spaghetti, a bemused Bigfoot

giggles from his spot in the trees. When they
drink the amber fluid from clear cylinders,
humans will destroy even their own nests.

The Ghost at the Bottom of the Well

Richard Brautigan sleeps fitfully in a suite
on the 35th floor of the Keio Plaza Hotel
in Tokyo. He awakens to the sound of whiskey

in his blood. It sounds like a thousand pickaxes
striking granite. He stands at the window
in his rosy kimono, gazing over an urban canyon

of high rises, horns, and giant billboards with
pictures of Barbara Streisand. He launches out
and flies towards Mount Fuji. He swoops in

to the Moss Temple in Kyoto, where he makes
a thousand wishes that will never come true.
It is 1976: Richard Brautigan's final flight.

Forced to ride the bullet train back to Tokyo,
he sits next to the window, his notebook open
on his lap, his pen tucked behind his ear.

The Japanese businessmen don't know how
to account for this tall, long-blond-haired man
in a rosy kimono taking up space on their

commuter train. Is he not a representative
of the race of warriors who sent apocalyptic
greetings to Hiroshima, to Nagasaki?

Brautigan can no longer scribble poems
into his notebook. As the beautiful scenery
passes him at a thousand miles per hour,

his ears fill with the sound of whiskey in
his blood. It sounds like the long, echoing cry
of a wounded creature at the bottom of a well.

Still Life with Winchester

Richard Brautigan balances the heavy weapon
in his shooting hand, aims at midnight, and fires.
You idiot, his wife Akiko yells, *there are children*

sleeping in this house! The other drunken men
around the kitchen table take turns putting
bullet holes in the big clock on the wall.

What more formidable enemy, after all,
than Time? *The children can sleep after*
we're dead, the men say. They gargle amber

and review their evening game of HORSE
under the driveway spotlight. Jim Harrison
prefers the short but fancy game inside the key —

the gyrating behind-the-back flip shot.
Tom McGuane is a distance man — hitting
set shots from nearly half court. Tallest,

Brautigan taunts his friends with cruel jokes
and sky hooks. The men jostle and bump
like young goats. Brautigan opens the heavy

cylinder; one by one, he slides more
bullets into the chambers of his heart;
he takes aim at the center of his life.

Neither Notebook nor Bottle

Richard Brautigan rocks in his big chair before
the picture window of his drafty house in Bolinas,
a settlement of the dead as much as the living.

The ghost of a Chinese woman, a former servant
in the house, resides on the third floor. Like all
who perch on seaside promontories, she finds solace

in the ebb and flow of the tide, the crash and
boom of the waves upon the rocks, the crack and
slide of Cypress trees as they break and fall into the sea.

A lone stag comes to feed on Richard Brautigan's
nasturtiums. He lowers his great head into the brush,
then raises up and turns his antlers like antenna

toward the horizon. At Brautigan's side is neither
notebook nor bottle. Only a loaded nickel-plated
Smith & Wesson on the small table at his elbow.

The house lists and creaks like a wooden ship.
The moon appears from behind the fog, takes
a seat at her instrument, tosses her locks back over

her shoulders, cracks her pale knuckles. She begins
to play Debussy's "Sunken Cathedral." Brautigan
leans his head back and rests his eyes. Upstairs

the ghost of the Chinese woman wanders
from room to room; her scuffling footsteps
whisper Richard Brautigan's secrets to the wind.

Beneath the Eucalyptus Beats an Ashen Heart

Richard Brautigan's ashes reside in a Japanese urn
buried beneath Eucalyptus in a cemetery
on the rocky California coast. Next to the small

churchyard stands a flock of sheep, staring out
to sea as Brautigan himself was wont to do.
These sheep are his eyes now, their hooves

his feet, their bleats his words. Richard Brautigan's
thoughts are now their thoughts. Day after day
they gaze out at the migrating gray whales,

who go back and forth, year after year,
on the longest-known commute on planet Earth —
north to feed in the icy krill-rich bays of Alaska,

south to birth calves in the warm waters of Baja.
They sing along the way songs of yearning,
songs of wounded delight, as they glide and sink

and rise, from time to time blowing free
from their sad, immense nostrils a spray
whose particles join the Pacific breeze, carrying

echoes of their sweet songs across the face
of the deep, consoling you, consoling me,
consoling the sheep next to the churchyard

as they look out to sea with Brautigan's eyes,
listen with Brautigan's ears, feel with Brautigan's
ashen heart beating there beneath the Eucalyptus.

Three

Hikers, Three Varieties

After Jeffrey Harrison

There are those for whom the mountain is just
one more fitness course made to work the quads
and boost the heart rate. Once they hit the peak,
they claim the view, comment on the weather,
compare pedometers. They can't stand still
for long lest their muscles begin to cool and cramp.
They can't wait to descend, to arrive at the coffee shop
in full regalia and check today's trail off their list.
For them, one switch-backed, fat-burning ascent
may very well be mistaken for another.

And there are those for whom the hike is a social
outing — a chance to walk their dogs and complain
of their lot: their inattentive spouse, their burdensome
children. When they finally stumble across the bench
in the clearing, Fido straining at the leash, tongue
lolling, they sit just long enough to water the animal and
ready the plastic baggie for collection. They've missed
the quail and white-tailed deer, the rattlesnake and
painted ladies flittering among trailside thistles.
No wild thought has intruded upon their day.

And then there are those lonesome fools for whom
the trail is a listening post on the universe. Attuned to
the daily office of blossom and rot, their ears are pricked up
for mystery borne upon the liquid rustle of summer leaves.
Their eyes wander towards the shadowy undergrowth,

the wagging branch, the tremendous wings slicing
across the sky. They break through at the startling peak
just as the breeze's lullaby chimes its final notes.
Stalked by some divine commotion, they gaze
over the fertile valley, speechless, attentive, still.

Awake at 3 A.M.

After Li Po

A chorus of crickets
in the zinnia bed.
Indifferent, the moon

shines her blue spotlight
on the plum tree, the grass,
the neighbor's shed.

What am I thinking?
I must've known when
I planted those zinnias

it would be like this.
Another jar of wine
and I'll be wise enough

to stop idle speculation
and take my part
in the insect choir.

When the Children Were Young

We often lived in the land
of Silly. We picked grapefruit
from the backyard tree and

lobbed them over home plate
in place of the Whiffle Ball.
Two or three swings and

someone would connect, whacking
the fruit across the lawn.
Often it broke open, little

yellow piñata, sending showers
of pulp and juice pinwheeling
across the sparse July grass.

The children were young and
we were young. Bath time
scrubbed away the day's debris.

Even then we thought, Oh,
let these days go on and on,
let summer stretch and yawn

and nap open-mouthed in
the big chaise lounge, a careless
snore in its freckled nose.

Local Habitations

Jacaranda is the tree for us, twice-blooming
in our region, a bold and fragrant purple in spring,
a paler but somehow richer blue in autumn.

Turn any corner in our neighborhood and see them
lined along the parkway in a conspiracy of beauty.
So we, in our youth, were given to the brave pose

or the startling proclamation. And now we have,
how shall I say it, deepened, taken on a subtle
complexity we could not in spring have imagined.

How strange and lovely to find ourselves in
this changing light. We pull the car over to the curb
to gawk in silence. The tree for us is Jacaranda.

Love Poem

Please me forever.

Hepburn my Tracy.
Bacall my Bogart.
Lucy my Desi.

Thisbe my Pyramus.
Isolde my Tristan.
Luthien my Beren.

Me forever please.

Laura my Petrarch.
Beatrice my Dante.
Elizabeth my Robert.

Alice my Gertrude.
Frida my Diego.
Joy my Jack.

Forever please me.

Josephine my Napoleon.
Clementine my Winston.
Bess my Harry.

Bathsheba my David.
Rachel my Jacob.
Eve my Adam.

Me please forever.

Guinevere my Lancelot.
Cleopatra my Antony.
Penelope my Odysseus.

Gracie my George.
Nora my Nick.
Costello my Abbott.

Please forever me.

Yoko my John.
Taylor my Burton.
June my Johnny.

Katie my Luther.
Victoria my Albert.
Heloise my Abelard.

Forever me please.

Jane my Tarzan.
Beauty my Beast.
Yin my Yang.

Fifi my Pepi.
Harriet my Ozzie.
Piggy my Kermit.

Please please please.
Me me me.
Forever forever forever.

Prayer for a Marriage

Welsh rebel Owen Glendower instructed
his longbow archers to dip the tips
of their arrows into their own feces.
That way, if the English Prince Mortimer's
troops survived the initial piercings,
they would soon find themselves mad
with fever and drowning in their own pus.

It wasn't enough the sting of your arrows
launched in that fight we had last week.
It was the festering infection they carried,
so that long after the barbs were removed,
the pain and nausea lingered. Worse,
I thrust my own shit-dipped
lance in a desperate counterattack.

In these skirmishes Ego must be protected
at all costs. Well, it is time to strip him
of his medals and expose his cowardice.
For too long the phony bastard has pretended
to be a warrior for truth. His absurd shield
and breastplate rust after the slightest rain,
and he can't even remember his own creed.

Enough! Take this pledge with me.
Let us snap his arrows one by one,
and walk the field of battle without
a care for who has won the day.
Let us sing a *Non nobis* and send that
mercenary creep halting to his bivouac,
trailing his quiver in the bloody mud.

After a Hard Rain

Last night we feared the wind
might blow the door down.
Like the wolf in the old story,
it huffed and puffed, tossing sheets
of water against the house.
It shook us from basement
to attic, windows rattling
in their casements. Thank God
everything held firm. This
morning's bright sun bounces
light off everything. Squinting,
I walk the yard, picking up
branches and shattered nests.
Around us this winter our friends
sicken and die. One by one
the diagnoses come in and
the treatment plans begin.
So far we've been to three
memorials, with more to come.
Some seasons come at you this way,
an unseen hand holds you to the mat:
Cry uncle. Go on, say it. Say uncle.
But this morning, as you braided
my hair, I had the feeling that
things might be turning. It'll be
Easter soon. This afternoon,
I'll go out and pick up the fallen
Ficus tree on the back patio.
Set it back in its place. Later

we'll drive up to the city for tea
with Malcolm and Heidi, then
Evensong at Grace Cathedral.
We'll break our Lenten fast
in the bar of the Huntington Hotel,
put Frank Sinatra on the Juke and
dance a slow whirl beneath dim lights.
I'm so grateful for you, my love,
and I wanted to say so while
it's calm and quiet, while my thoughts
are clear, and the light is so pure, before
the fog rolls in, or the rain comes again.

Rats in the Attic

They are having a raucous party up there.
It is a rainy night. My wife is out of town.
The cat and I occupy opposite ends of the big bed.
She lifts her head as I stir. It is a rainy night,
and these roof rats have found a way in.
They've been eating the oranges on the backyard tree
and scampering atop the wooden fence at dusk.
Now they have come inside with fruit sugar
surging through their tiny blood vessels.
The cat yawns and stretches. Soon her eyes close.
The rats are dancing the Macarena in my attic!
After a brief fantasy of setting the whole place
ablaze, I grab the remote control. I discover
an old Hitchcock movie on TCM. Eventually
the sweet cadence of Cary Grant's lilting voice
soothes me, and I settle some pillows and enjoy
the background music of rain upon the window.
Cary and Grace Kelly make out on a divan
in the Italian Riviera with fireworks bursting
over the yacht harbor. I drift off for a while and awaken
as TCM host Ben Mankiewicz notes the irony
of Princess Grace's tragic death along the very roads
driven in the movie. The rain has stopped.
The cat is snoring. The rats have settled into
the pillowy insulation overhead. I move to
the window just in time to watch the clouds part
and the sun come up over Cupertino, California!

Summer School

Well, it's final. It's settled. I'm not going
to the UK this summer. I will not
ride the rickety train from Edinburgh
to London. I will not wander through
the old Roman spa town of Bath, sing
Evensong in its splendid Abbey, nor drive
a rental car on the wrong side of the road
to Wales. I won't be hiking the rocky hills
above the seaside capital of Cardiff.

Instead I will teach a six-week Introduction
to Poetry to bored community college students.
Rather than fish for trout in an icy Highlands
stream, or turn my flimsy California collar
up against the winds of the Salisbury plains,
I will recite for my students "The Lake Isle
of Innisfree" while they text to one another:
"can u believe this boring old fart?
he really *likes* the odor of this moldy shit!"

I will not arise and go to the UK. Rather
I will ride my bike in the heat of a sweltering
drought and sip iced tea at Starbucks and
scribble into my notebook, recording not
the ruddy cheeks and throaty dialects of the Welsh,
nor their love for community choirs and football
and ale and turtleneck sweaters, nor their
bemusement at right-wing American politicians
and baby-faced Silicon Valley billionaires.

At night I will consume ever-increasing
gobs of mint chocolate chip ice cream
(which my doctor has warned me against)
and calculate just how much of my summer
paycheck goes toward my children's mortgage-
sized college loans. I will fall asleep to the
charmless banalities of late-night blue-light
talk shows which, like this dreary summer,
like this very poem, pass without distinction.

Drought Orison

Against a darkening sky
willow branches droop,
droop down; stringy limbs
sway like a half-drunk sax player
awaiting his solo, sway because
something stirs in the roots, sending
a tingle up the fibrous trunk.
The leaves glimmer and turn,
turn light to dark, dark to light,
like a school of sardines,
like a young girl who shakes
the rain from her hair and
lets it fall, fall from her touch.

Meanwhile the young man
at the Goodyear store
on the corner pushes a dolly
loaded with display tires
across the lot, and the hound
with its head out the window
of the truck rounding the corner
barks five barks at the raindrops
only now beginning to fall.
Who's to say that the lightening
sparking and forking, sparking
and forking across the valley
right now isn't a response
to the willow's fervent call?

Day Hike

Dew still glistening in the undergrowth, Brother Lewis
and I trudge up the winding trail. Our morning legs
carry us at a steady pace. In branches overhead, jays
and squirrels chip-chap their tedious political argument.
With nonpartisan ears, we listen to their chatter.

Our breathing grows labored as we ascend, stepping
over roots and rocks, watching for snakes. Our pace slows.
Twice we are surprised by does forging a new path
to the creek. Now and then we break through gaps
in the oaks and pause to watch the hawks circling the peak.

Oak gives way to pine. Buzzards patrol the ravine where
a solitary horse whinnies. At one of the switchbacks,
our view opens and the sky turns bright. The sun
meanders across the afternoon sky, none too eager to arrive.
Which saint was it who stared at the sun without going blind?

On the limestone tonsure at the top of the mountain,
Brother Lewis and I sit on a bench overlooking the bay.
We trade gulps from our water bottle. Lewis tugs at his
cassock to cool his skin. His bare feet are caked with clay.
A contemplative lizard tops the bench and shares our view.

In the distance, the bridge's long sweeping span, suspended
between mighty towers, appears small. Beside it rises
the city named for Francis, its famous skyline welcoming
the evening sun like a prodigal sibling. And spread across
the valley just beneath us: second-generation silicon geniuses.

The lizard completes his liturgy and scrambles into the weeds.
What are you feeling? asks Brother Lewis. *Gratitude,* I reply.
Gratitude, he echoes. I half ask, *Maybe we should pray?*
Gazing over the fertile valley once named for Clare,
Lewis says, *Isn't that what we've been doing all along?*

How to Paint Clouds

The secret is not to think of them
as clouds. Simply lay down your sky.

Let it dry. Empty your brain of clouds.
Load your most ragged brush with paint:

drag it through the Titanium White,
dip into Cerulean Blue, then a touch

of Payne's Gray; add just a skosh
of Cadmium Yellow or Magenta.

Let your arm be a painter's arm:
blend, swirl, dab — make the canvas hum.

Find shadows, deepen. With just the corner
of your brush, play among the highlights.

Stop before you're finished. Don't muddy
your clouds with too many strokes.

How can they drift if anchored by work?
Surrender them to wind and whim.

A painted sky should invite us
to zip up our jackets and fly.

Getting the Moon Right

It's less a matter of perception than of composition.
A moon in the center is a distortion of her place
in our lives: she is powerful but she is peripheral.
Her draw resides in her aloofness — obscured by

the leaves of a yew or the sharp corner of a skyscraper
or the frame of a rotting window. Only a few nights
in a given year do we stop in our tracks and gape
and point. More often, she lingers over our shoulder

in her gray nightgown and ragged slippers, curlers
dangling from her newly-washed hair. Nevertheless,
when she whispers to us in her gravely come hither voice
(come back to bed my darling, I grow cold without you)

we follow her into the corners of the languid night;
we follow her into the lonely crevices of our dreams.

Cantankerous

Today something's come over me —
something's lurking in my shadows,
ready to pounce. I feel feisty
and edgy and fixed to fight.
I'm thinking of the old, bald monk
whose books I've been reading
and whose funny, wise videos
I've been watching on YouTube.
Such a kind man with such a kind
message about a kind God and His
kind gospel of love for all beings.
Well, I'm sick of it, you see.
I don't want to listen to anymore
love talk today. I'm sick of
the sticky goodness of such babble.

I tell you something's come over me.
Today I want to flush an M80 down
a public toilet and hear the echoing
boom and watch water gush and
smoke billow and people's astonished
faces at my bad behavior. *What's with*
that jerk? they'd no doubt say.
What kind of selfish prick would pull
such a prank? Isn't he the guy posting
Dalai Lama quotes all over Facebook?
I knew it all along. These religious types —
hypocrites, grifters, and sex fiends all.
The sooner exposed the better.
True! I might shout. *True, every word!*
You'd better steer clear of me today.

Something's really come over me.
I'm skipping my meditation.
I'm ready to chuck all my books
into the street and light them up
in a huge bonfire, dance naked
around the red, yellow, and blue flames.
I'm likely to pee in your prize petunias,
butter your toast with my vitriolic snot.
I think I'll shave my head and tattoo
a swastika on my nose. Oh, I'm rolling
towards the cliff edge at a high rate of speed.
I may just be a danger to myself
and others. You may in fact need to call
the men in white coats to take me away
because something's come over me today.

Auto Bison

He has spent his life
in parking lots.

He has warmed his hands
on radiator grills

the way cave men
stood around fire.

With only minor design
and color variations,

the same cars have been
circling him for decades.

They sputter and growl.
They move like herd animals

on the Great Plains.
They are shells containing

soft and vulnerable organisms,
who imagine themselves

creatures of consequence.
But the cars know better.

They keep circling;
on occasion, just to see

if he is paying attention,
they blow their great horns.

Four

To Catch a Nebbish

He	Um. Is this seat taken?
She	It's yours if your name be
	Farnsworth Bellybottom.
He	No one's ever guessed my name.
She	Well, don't just stand there.
	Plop your foolish little
	Bellybottom on this stool.
He	I'm going to say something
	very un-Farnsworthian:
	Come with me to the reservoir.
She	Only if you'll let me drive.
He	Uh.
She	Don't think. Decide.
He	Will you take the turns slow?
She	I could promise, but —
He	Do you know the Hitchcock film
	where Cary Grant and Grace Kelly —
She	You're trying too hard —
He	Drive atop the curvy cliffs
	of Monaco, tires squealing —
She	You blew it. I hate movies.
He	I hide my eyes during that scene.
She	The call dropped. The line is dead.
He	Let me at least take
	a fortifying drink or two.
She	Give me your keys, cowboy.
He	I've never done this before.
She	Spare me the movie clichés.
	We're on our way, lover.

He   You're stealing me, aren't you?

She Forward march, pilgrim.

He   Lead on, future Mrs. Bellybottom.

Harvest Moon

He	Come out and look at her!
She	I see, she's swollen with honey.
He	Time for the great reaping.
She	Time for you and time for me.
He	She won't let me sleep tonight.
She	She tugs at the tidal blood.
He	A few ancient societies
	followed a lunar calendar.
She	Why would you do otherwise?
He	Those on the solar calendar:
	warlike, ambitious, acquisitive.
She	Are you making this up?
He	What do I really know and
	what do I merely think I know?
She	The moon, she knows.
	That's all that matters.
He	She's just a pale rock reflecting
	the sun's roiling cauldron.
She	Sometimes the truth is ugly.
He	Well, then, maybe that's not true.
She	She's so beautiful tonight
	I feel she might burst.
He	What was it Keats said
	about truth and beauty?
She	He said shut up and kiss.

Clowder Cloister

He	Tell me about the nunnery.
She	Convent. It was marvelous.
He	Yeah, but — Did you flunk out?
She	They suggested the communal life might not be for me. After some thought, I agreed.
He	Sounds like an amicable divorce.
She	Best break-up I ever had.
He	I wonder how ours will go.
She	You're already imagining our end?
He	Will it come with bang or whimper?
She	We'll end with a whimpering bang.
He	I'd almost prefer a banging whimper, if an end must come.
She	All things must pass away.
He	But back to the nunnery.
She	Convent. What about it?
He	Do you still keep the Hours?
She	In my modified little way.
He	Does God watch over you?
She	She keeps an eye on us all.
He	Even ex-nuns? Even reprobates like me? Whatever for?
She	Therein lies the mystery — What deity in its right mind would give a hang for us?
He	Only a very lonely or a very co-dependent creator would persevere with this crazy mess.

She   She's like the cat lady
        on my street who takes in
        all the strays, rejecting none.

He   And that's what a nunnery is —
        a home for wayward felines.

She   It's called a convent. And
        God floats the vet bills for
        the entire flea-bedeviled world.

Man Bites Dog

He   The American Pit Bull
Terrier is bred to kill.
That bruiser there could
easily chomp a baby.

She   Big dogs are muzzled
for damn good reason.

He   235 pounds of pressure
in those jaws right there.
Ever seen a muzzled
crocodile? Duct tape.
They wrap the snout
round and round with it.

She   How could duct tape
hold their big traps shut?

He   All their strength is in
the muscles that snap
the jaws closed, not
those that yawn open.

She   Remember that croc
in Peter Pan? Tic toc.
How many pounds exerted
in your bite, dear?

He   I can't compete with
the pit bull or the croc.
All my strength, such as
it is, lay in my mind.

She   And what a mind.

He   The better to eat you
with, my dainty dear.

She   Devour me, please.
He   First you must unbuckle
       the muzzle round my thoughts.

Foot Massage

He	I love your cute little toes.
She	They're all yours for now.
He	Your heels are dry and cracked.
She	They're so ugly. But I'm counting on you to love them. The lotion is so soothing. Can you do this forever, please?
He	Even this would turn to torture.
She	How could such pleasure turn?
He	Everything ripens then rots, sweetens then sours. It's the nature of things.
She	Let's test it. Keep rubbing.
He	My hands are getting sore. Soon my attention will wane.
She	Will your love for me likewise one day dry up and crack?
He	We'll have to keep the lotion on hand. Now ... how's that?
She	Rub right along the tendon there. Hey, is it over already?
He	My turn.
She	Yes, of course. Such elegant toes for a man.
He	Hold out your hands. There.
She	Mmm. That's cool and creamy. Prop them right here on my milky white thighs.
He	Ease into it now. The feet have no fat to protect them.

She	Look how this toe leans into his brother. They can't bear to be apart, these two.
He	I take it all back. There's no way such pleasure could turn to pain.
She	Speak for yourself. Already my hands are beginning to cramp and tire and ache.
He	Rub me to Nirvana, baby.
She	It's easy to wax metaphysical when the pleasure is yours.
He	Let's stop talking. That's quite enough wisdom for one day.
She	Shall I hum a little tune?
He	Now silence. Keep rubbing. More lotion. Keep rubbing.

Mating Ritual

She   Brush your teeth, carnivore.

He   I can't find the condoms.

She   You've been eating the flesh
of innocent animals; you disgust me.

He   I just bought a new box;
they were right in this drawer.

She   I said brush your teeth.

He   What have you done with them?

She   I threw them in the river.

He   There are no rivers around here.

She   I tossed them over the cliff.

He   No, really. What have you done?

She   I swallowed them one by one.
Now brush your teeth
and drop your pants.

No Problem

She	Are you letting your beard grow?
He	I don't know. Should I?
She	It makes you look older.
	You've gone salt and pepper.
He	Supposed to be distinguished.
She	I have no problem with that.
	I just don't want to
	wake up next to Gandalf.
He	How about, say, Sean Connery?
She	How is your Scots brogue these days?
He	I've got a wee problem w' that.
	You've a spot of gray heather
	on the hill yourself, lassie.
She	Are you planning to seduce me
	with insults? Because I think
	in that case I prefer Gandalf.
He	You must return this ring to
	the evil fire of its forging.
She	Put that back on, wizard.
He	I have no problem with that.
She	If I hear you're cavorting with
	hobbits, I'll shave you myself.
He	I have a problem with that.
She	Bring any dwarves home and
	I'll go live with the elves.
He	I have no problem with elves,
	although I suspect their sexuality
	may be more complicated than ours.

She   I'm willing to suspend judgment.
       It's the orcs I cannot abide.
He   Sorry-ass thugs of Middle-earth.
She   We're agreed then. The orcs
       can go fuck themselves.
He   I have no problem with
       orcs fucking only themselves.
She   Shall we pay the bill
       and proceed to Lothlorien?
He   I have a slight problem with that.
       I am terrified of heights.
She   You know, the ethereal music
       of Lothlorien grates my nerves.
He   I'm not entirely comfortable
       with all the mind-reading
       that goes on in that realm.
She   However, I have always loved
       archery. Sport of kings — and queens.
He   I've got arrows in my quiver
       if you can provide a target.
She   On that point, my dear, I am
       entirely without a problem.

Household Pairs

He	Why do you leave your earrings all over the place?
She	I do that, don't I?
He	Here's a pair on the old telephone table. Remember when the telephone was a household thing rather than a pocket thing or a purse thing?
She	Do they match? Are they red?
He	And here's another pair on the kitchen counter.
She	It's that Puck again — up to his usual tricks. Better check to see if the milk has soured.
He	Here's the swirly green and blue pair in the fruit bowl.
She	It must be spring. I'm shedding earrings.
He	There's a single in the bathroom right next to the soap.
She	So noted. One stray next to the soap.
He	I came across those feathery dangles you were looking for — Let's see … where? … the cup holder in the passenger seat?

She	Tell me if you find the silver and turquoise turtles I got in Maui last Christmas.
He	Don't tell me the turtles have gone.
She	Just like the real ones, they swam off into the deep blue.

Emotional Water-boarding

She She told him everything.
He Why would she do that?
She She couldn't continue with
     a heartful of secrets, she said.
He So she unloaded the truth.
     What was his reaction?
She He sat down and cried.
He Well, of course he did.
     I'll tell you what he
     should have done though.
She He shook like a wet puppy.
He He should have shot her.
She Somebody should have shot her
     a long time ago, shot her dead.
He Anybody with that much
     hostility or meanness or hate —
She Then she packed her things
     and hopped a flight to Vegas.
He Wait. Did she tell him
     about the child in Atlanta?
She And the bass player
     who fathered the Atlanta child.
     Also, the drugged-up cyclist.
He She told him all then.
She Or practically all. What
     motivated her confession?
He Something utterly cruel in her.
She I'm glad we agree on this.
He We utterly agree on this.

She	Do you have anything you'd like to tell me now?
He	You mean any secrets to divulge? Not a chance in the world.
She	They're locked in the vault?
He	I've long ago forgotten the combination. And you?
She	I also have enough secrets to blacken a human heart.
He	Secrets you will forever hold?
She	Not even Donald Rumsfeld could torture a confession through these sealed lips.
He	What if I urinated on your sacred text?
She	Even pee-soaked scripture and a dose of Pentothal wouldn't wrangle it from me.
He	"Where ignorance is bliss, 'tis folly to be wise."
She	Fa-la-la-la folly, folly to be wise.

Natural Selection

She   I came upon your son today
peeling the wings from a Monarch.

He   Was the insect already dead?

She   What does that matter?

He   If he caught it to kill, then
he's taking after you.

She   You're saying I'm a killer?

He   Natural born. You've been plotting
my demise since you caught me.

She   Today might be a good day
for you to die, sweetheart.

He   If he found it already dead,
then he's taking after me.

She   Hold still. This won't hurt a bit.

He   It's all one big science
experiment, this life.

She   Or should I say it'll
hurt me more than you?

He   I'm more Blue Morpho
than Monarch, and you —

She   Quit your wiggling now.

He   You're our lovely Painted Lady.

She   Hold still now, sweet daddy,
while I peel your body from its soul.

No Diva She

She   Your lover called again.

He   I wish you'd stop saying that.
         It's not funny, you know.

She   I can hear her breathing on the line.

He   I don't have a lover.
         There's only you and you alone.

She   She's a coward, your tootsie.
         Tell her to speak up.

He   If I had a tootsie,
         she wouldn't be a coward.

She   Tell her to drop by, your
         floozie-woozie. Tell her to
         come up and see me sometime.

He   Who are you, Mae West?

She   I'll Mae her West, my dear.
         And then I'll Mae yours.

He   You're so hot when you're jealous.

She   This is no jealous act.
         I'm no soap opera diva.

He   No one could accuse you
         of being a diva, my love.

She   Damn straight. No diva me.
         Tell her what I said.

He   What? Tell her what?

She   Nevermind. I'll tell her
         myself next time she calls.

He   There won't be a next time.
         There wasn't a first time.

She　Bring it over here, Big Boy.

He　You're not going to hurt me?

She　If I do, you'll beg for more.
　　　You may approach. Come.

With a Little Help from Van Gogh

He   What would you think if I
       brought you my severed ear —
       would you throw it
       right back in my face?

She   What is your hypothetical
       motivation — love or hostility?

He   It's a token of radical devotion:
       what says I love you more
       than violent dismemberment?

She   Is this ear dripping with fresh
       blood or cleaned and freeze-dried?

He   Why? What does that matter?

She   It might be hard to disguise
       my disgust; I get queasy
       when I merely stub my toe.

He   Very well, the ear is clean
       and my wound cauterized.

She   And bandaged?

He   And bandaged.

She   Then I might be able to receive it
       in the spirit in which it is offered.
       But what to do with it?

He   It's already pierced. Hang it
       from a fine gold chain.

She   Let it dangle next to my heart? Oh,
       please. Why an ear? — it's been done.

He   You complain I don't listen:
       what more evocative symbol —
       my constant ear to your heart?

She   Here's a test of your radical devotion:
            for evocative symbolism,
            nothing says love like a penis.

He   Wouldn't you rather a personalized tattoo?

She   How quaint. How bourgeois.

He   Your likeness in permanent ink.

She   Where is my Ginsu knife?

He   Would you settle for a ring?

She   What a conversation piece:
            "Is that a penis I see
            swinging between your breasts?"

He   I thought you were disgusted
            by fresh blood and mutilation.

She   I'll merely hand you the sharpened
            blade, then I'll turn my back.

He   Like a royal Mayan sacrifice?
            But then how would we —

She   Perhaps like a lizard's tale
            you'd grow a new one.

He   Van Gogh was crazy, you know, but
            it was Gaugin who drove him there.

She   Gaugin was the very model
            of sanity — just look at his nudes.

He   Don't stand and walk out on me!

She   Cries the Queen of Hearts:
            "Off with his head!"

Bitter/Sweet

She   Are you going to finish that?

He   No. Would you like it?

She   Only if you're finished.

He   I am now. It's yours.

She   Thank you. You're sure?

He   I'm sure of so little now.
        But I want you to have it.

She   I love meekness in a man.
        A little deference goes far.

He   I've changed my mind.

She   What? You can't do that.
        I've begun to salivate.

He   Turn off the faucet.

She   Give me that. I need it.

He   I love decisiveness in a woman.
        Decisiveness bordering on desperation.

She   You're about to get smacked.

He   Desperation bordering on anger.
        Anger boiling over into violence.

She   Give me that cookie
        and nobody gets hurt.

He   Hurt upon hurt upon hurt.
        What's one more black eye?

She   Fine. I don't want it now.

He   Here. It's all yours.

She   You've ruined it. Why
        do you have to ruin everything?

He   Mmm. Delicious. The last bite
        is always the best bite.

She	Bastard.
He	Bitch.
She	Asshole.
He	Cunt.
She	You can't pull the 'c' word.
	You've no right to it.
He	I'm sorry. I went too far.
She	Way too fucking far —
	Where are you going?
He	To buy you a new cookie.
She	It better have chocolate
	in it, and lots of it.
He	Coming right up, dear.
She	I'll have a coffee, too.
	And a shot of whiskey.
	Kidding. Chocolate'll do it.
He	Are we good?
She	Oh, we're good.
He	No, I mean really.
	Are we really good?
She	We're unbelievably good.

Put Some Bleachers Out in the Sun

She	Here's a song to drive by.
He	Keep your eyes on the road.
She	They work better in their
	sockets, where they belong.
He	You can't dance and drive.
She	Hey, turn that back on!
He	Only if you settle down
	and focus on your driving.
She	I'm driving just fine.
He	You're all over the highway!
She	Dude, it's a big highway.
	Plenty of room for lateral action.
He	There's a point at which lateral
	action impedes forward progress.
She	Who died and made you
	god of forward progress?
He	Just pull over here, please.
She	If you want out, jump.
He	You're crossing the yellow line.
She	You crossed it a few minutes ago.
He	All right. This just isn't funny.
She	It's hilarious. Ready to jump?
He	Can't you see I've been lonely?
She	It'll be a nice, easy roll
	from here into that ditch.
He	Said Second Mother to Seventh Son.
She	Here, let me get the door for you.
	Watch out for that tumbleweed.

I'll See You in My Dreams

She	You won't find anyone who does what I do.
He	No doubt that's true. You are truly unique.
She	You really are such a —
He	Bastard, I know, and also a jerk, an ass, a —
She	At least leave me the pleasure of cussing you out.
He	Sorry, I owe you that much.
She	That much and so much more. You'll never see me again.
He	I'll see you even when I don't see you. You're part of me and I'm part —
She	Stop with the platitudes! You're no part of me.
He	I'll pop into your mind when you least expect it.
She	You will not haunt me. Go right now. Walk away.
He	Into the sunset he canters on the black and white pony.
She	You're not getting custody.
He	Face it now, sweetie: that boy was only a dream.
She	What the hell are you saying?
He	I'm filling dead air. I'm terrified of silence.

She   Walk away. Go right now.
He   Is this a bang or a whimper?
She   It's just the end.
      Or at least the beginning
      of the bitter end.
He   Endings are never sweet.
She   Only sickeningly so.
      Walk now. Go.

Acknowledgments

The author is grateful to the editors of the following publications, where some of these poems first appeared:

Atlanta Review: "When the Children Were Young"

California Quarterly: "Awake at 3 A.M.," "Colony Collapse Disorder," "Household Pairs," "Strong Umbrellas," "How to Paint Clouds"

Canary: "Suburban Scene"

The Carolina Quarterly: "Bitter/Sweet"

Catamaran Literary Reader: "Zen and the Art of Loneliness"

Chariton Review: "Pineapple Wedges That Just Keep Coming"

Chiron Review: "Blue Plate Special for the Whole Wide World," "The Owl Follows the River to Paradise," "Torch Song for Peter Lorre"

Clare: "Headlines from a Private Tabloid"

Hotel Amerika: "Man Bites Dog," "Natural Selection," "No Problem"

Iodine Poetry Journal: "Woman in a Purple Coat"

Naugatuck River Review: "Neither Notebook Nor Bottle"

Palooka: "Baudelaire Buzzes the Gorilla Compound," "Walking with Wordsworth, Punching with Papa," "Weeping a Mote Around Ben Franklin," "With the Devil You Never Know"

Parabola: "Day Hike," awarded Honorable Mention in the Thomas Merton Poetry of the Sacred contest, 2015

Perfume River Poetry Review: "Korah, Son of Izhar," "New Philosophy"

Rattle: "Apocalyptic Charlton Heston"

San Diego Poetry Annual: "Summer School," awarded Third Place in The Steve Kowit Poetry Prize, 2016

San Pedro River Review: "The Absinthe Drinkers"

Slipstream: "Body Double," "Zig-zagging Down Lombard
    Street," which was also published as a broadside by The
    Center for Book Arts, New York
Spillway: "Devouring Marilyn," "Mating Ritual," "Our Groovy
    West Coast Necropolis," "Still Life with Winchester"
Still Point Arts Quarterly: "Day Hike"
Third Thursday: "Local Habitations"

The author would also like to thank Ken Weisner, Bob
Dickerson, Jill Quigley, Amanda Williamsen, Dorianne
Laux, Dana Gioia, Ron Koertge, and Christine Cote for their
encouragement, editorial wizardry, and friendship during the
making of these poems.

About the Author

David Denny is the author of the Shanti Arts short story collection, *The Gill Man in Purgatory*, as well as three previous poetry collections: *Man Overboard, Fool in the Attic,* and *Plebeian on the Front Porch*. His poems and short stories have appeared in numerous journals and magazines, including *The Sun, Narrative, Catamaran, Rattle*, and *Parabola*. He holds an M.F.A. degree from the University of Oregon and an M.A.T. from Fuller Theological Seminary. Recent awards and honors include The Thomas Merton Poetry of the Sacred Contest, The Steve Kowit Poetry Prize, The Center for Book Arts Broadside Award, an Artist Laureate Award from the Silicon Valley Arts Council, numerous Pushcart nominations, and inaugural Poet Laureate of Cupertino, California. Denny is Professor of English at De Anza College and former editor of *Bottomfish* magazine.
— more information at daviddenny.net

SHANTI ARTS

art · nature · spirit

Please visit us on online

to browse our entire book catalog,

including additional poetry collections and fiction,

books on travel, nature, healing, art,

photography, and more.

www.shantiarts.com

CPSIA information can be obtained
at www.ICGtesting.com
Printed in the USA
LVHW020858290319
612266LV00006BA/85/P